MIDDLE SCHOOL
HIGH SCHOOL
COLLEGE & BEYOND

Carole Marsh's CAREERS CURRICULUM

Business ETHICS & ETIQUETTE for STUDENTS

You MUST Know These!

CAROLE MARSH

The real world of business is one of constant decisions, missteps, upsets, lost opportunities and more...unless you are well-versed in how to conduct yourself. This may be the most helpful book a young adult can read.

Carole Marsh's

CAREERS CURRICULUM™

Editor: Janice Baker
Assistant Editors: Charles Peterson
Madeline Vogler
Adrianna Atkinson
Cover Design: Lisa Kelly
Content Design: Randolyn Friedlander
Lisa Kelly
Maggie Bowers
Project Manager: Paige Muh

For additional information about Carole Marsh's Careers Curriculum or other curriculum products, contact:

Gallopade International
P.O. Box 2779
Peachtree City, Georgia 30269
800-536-2438, ext. 11
www.careerscurriculum.com
www.gallopade.com

Carole Marsh's CAREERS CURRICULUM™

Books

Essential Skills for the Real World of Work:
Things *Every* Student Must Know!

Job Tracks: 60* Great Careers—and How to Get from Where You Are...to Where You Want to Go! *Real Job Success Stories from 21st Century Career Pathways!

Would *You* Hire This Person?: A Look at Getting Hired (or Not!)... from the Point of View of Your (Possible!) Future Employer

The Parent and Teacher's Guide to Helping Students Navigate the Bumpy Road from School to More School, First Job, and Career

Business Ethics and Etiquette for Students—
You MUST Know These!

WORK WORDS: Job/Business/Career Words and Terms You Need to Know!

Also available in ebook formats

Contents

Section 2: Etiquette 39

A Word from the Author

Ethics & Etiquette.

Ethics and Etiquette is not a rock band.

Ethics and etiquette are hard though, hard to imagine as interesting and fun and having anything to do with getting a job.

But, really, ethics and etiquette are this: ESSENTIAL JOB SKILLS.

Ethics pervade our lives, from personal and family...to school and community life...to work and careers, as you'll learn in this book. Ethics may seem invisible and behind the scenes, the land of lawyers and legal stuff, but that's not so.

Etiquette does the same thing...it affects our lives each and every day, and it's something people see about us constantly; no hiding behind the scenes here!

Two things can trip you up on your pathway to adulthood, advanced schooling, and your first job search and eventual career: yeah—ethics and etiquette. As you'll learn in this book, you care a lot more about these two subjects than you ever knew, and, your potential employer cares a LOT. You can bring a great education to the job interview table, and even a charming personality, but if you do not bring strong values and an acceptable degree of social behavior, your very character is in question, and your likelihood of being hired is greatly reduced.

Some things qualify as "insider secrets." So let's say that many of the things you'll learn here have never come up in school, but are things that if you learn, will help you immensely all your life.

I had to make three ethical decisions before breakfast, and then have breakfast with a group of people from the global business community, so my etiquette had to be perfect.

Ethics and Etiquette—two skills for success to help you rock on in the business world!

Go get em!

Carole Marsh

ETHICS is knowing the difference between what you have a right to do and what is right to do.

—Potter Stewart,
former Associate Justice of the United States Supreme Court

Section 1: Ethics

What the Heck *Are* Ethics?

You could describe *ethics* a lot of ways:

The dictionary says an *ethic* is a pretty-much-agreed-on idea about how a group of people should behave.

Ethics reflect how we think people should act. We think some things they do are good and ok, and some are bad and not at all right.

A code of ethics is a system of values that each and every member of a particular group abides by. For example, a doctor knows that no matter whether or not she is "at work," it's her duty to help anyone at any time if a medical situation arises. In olden days, knights lived by a code that promoted good deeds and frowned upon wrongdoings. Today, sometimes we worry we'll get sued if we try to help a car wreck victim, and hurt them instead. You could call this an "ethical dilemma."

Your ethics may keep you from telling your parents a lie because you think you should always be honest and tell the truth—*even if it might get you in trouble.*

Law vs. Ethics

Law is simply what is legal—what the government says you can and cannot do. Many laws are meant to protect what is ethical—laws can be bent and twisted, but a good code of ethics can be a shelter in a storm of uncertainty and doubt.

Ethics, put in a word-nutshell, is "doing the *right* thing." Our society today might still be segregated black and white if Civil Rights pioneers hadn't challenged the law with a higher authority: the ethics of human rights. Think about way back when our country was young, around the American Revolutionary War—we wouldn't be Americans today if we hadn't stuck to our guns, literally, and stood up for what we thought was fair and just. In business terms, England (the bully boss) wasn't giving the colonies (the employees) their rightful voice—remember "no taxation without representation?" Leave it to us to speak up by turning the Massachusetts Bay into an oversized teacup. Our country was built on this kind of rebellious, but ethical, behavior.

I don't recommend you go coloring on the walls at work, claiming it's your right to free speech, but what I'm suggesting is plain and simple... stay legitimate, lawful, and legal, but apply what you know is right to your everyday school, home, and work situations. Let ethics guide your business practices and see that good comes from good.

Everyday Ethics

It's pretty easy for us to understand personal ethics. It's even easy to figure out that it might be best to avoid hauling off and hitting someone, not just because it's wrong, but also because they'd probably clobber us back!

So how do we get our ideas about what's ethical and what's not? Ethics are handed down from parent to child, from generation to generation. Fortunately, most people think it's absolutely wrong to kill someone, to steal, to lie, to cheat, and other such clear-cut things. But where many of us see black and white, there are a lot more than "50 shades" of gray to compound the ethics issues and to confound our thoughts about them.

We see that the world works much better if we adhere to generally accepted moral and ethical standards of behavior. But our ethics may not be the same as someone else's ethics. Different people, families, countries, and cultures have different ethics. Big game hunters may not think it's ethical to hunt lions with grenades and tanks — only guns are a fair fight. But animal rights people may feel that killing the lion at all is completely unethical.

You may think that it's ethical to tell a little white lie to keep from upsetting someone you love, but your mom may not think that's ethical at all. (Especially if the LWL was that you *almost* passed English…when the truth is that you actually made an F-!)

Ethics has always been about good and bad, right and wrong. Not only what we do, but how we do it and *why* we do it.

Business Ethics

Once you get a job, you may discover that other people may not have the same ethics as you do. Yes, you may both agree that stealing is wrong. Absolutely. Positively. But, you may discover that they don't think there is anything wrong with taking home the company's paper clips, rubber bands, note pads, pens, and pencils.

"That's stealing!" you say. *"That stuff belongs to the business. They bought it and paid for it. It is not anyone's to take."*

"Aw, they've got more rubber bands than they know what to do with!" the other person argues. *"Besides, I do some work at home, so I need this stuff. I'm not* **really** *stealing."*

What do you think? This is not like stealing a car (or is it?!). No one will get caught or go to jail. But is it wrong? And if it is, what's the difference between stealing a car and rubber bands (no smart-alec answer here, please!)? If you owned the business, how do you think you would feel if someone ripped-off items you had paid for? Is there a time that it really would be ok to take such items home? How many? For how long? Even the ethics of paper clip filching can seem confounding. Or is it?

You begin to see the problem! Sometimes it seems like ethics is BLACK and WHITE. We don't steal cars. But sometimes it seems like ethics can be one big gray area. Is it ok to steal milk and bread from your rich neighbor for a hungry baby if you don't have any money? To lend a borrower money when you know they can't possibly repay it? To lie in an ad because you got paid to do so? And a million other things…

You can see how ethics can be different for different people. Or different at different times. Or different under different circumstances.

But isn't right *right* and wrong *wrong*?
What do you think?

Ethics Flavors

We have ethics that relate to every aspect of our behavior. There are business ethics, political ethics, medical ethics, and most anything else you can name.

Ethics can go by many names: values, morals, etiquette, good conduct, deportment, professionalism, or fair play.

"But where are the *rules*?" you might ask. "I don't see them written down anywhere."

You're right. We write down the rules of basketball. And we write out our laws. We write out the Boy Scout motto. And we write the Ten Commandments. We write down many things of this type, but there is no big book called *ETHICS*.

So, how are we supposed to know how to behave when it comes to these big gray areas? That's a good question. The truth probably is that most of the time we really *do* know how to act. We really *can* tell right from wrong. Things really *are* black and white, but sometimes we want something so bad that we begin to see a cloud of gray and we make choices that are *not* ethical—and then we try to make them sound like they *are* ethical.

Why would we do this?

Laziness — *"It was easier to take home the company's paper clips than to buy my own."*

Greed — *"It's not fair the company has all those rubber bands & I don't even have one!"*

To get even — *"The boss docked me an hour's pay for being late, but I'll show him, I'll steal five dollars worth of office supplies."*

Confusion — *"I guess it's ok to take home the stuff I need to work. I won't ask anyone if it's ok. I'll just do it."*

Power — *"It's my job & my desk & I can take this home if I want to."*

Complacency — *"Everyone else takes stuff home, so I might as well."*

As you can see, there are as many reasons as you can think of, even if they are unethical reasons. Toby Keith, country music superstar, borrowed a little anonymous quotation that speaks volumes about ethics:

> **"Ain't no right way**
> **To do the wrong thing."**

We all justify little wrongdoings by claiming good intentions or rationalizing situations to fit our needs—"I didn't steal—I was borrowing."—but that doesn't make it right.

Ethics Basics

Wouldn't you agree that lying, cheating, and stealing are wrong? The easy part is this: Almost all instances of being unethical can be tied back to one of those three actions. In business, specific names are given to different types of the same unethical actions. For example, when you steal what someone has written in a book, it is called plagiarism. Listed below are examples of different ways businesspeople lie, steal, and cheat.

Lying: breaking contracts (promises), slander and libel, fraud, and money laundering

Stealing: copyright infringement, intellectual property theft, unfair supply chains, and plagiarism

Cheating: partisan partnerships, buddy favoritism, bribery, kickbacks, insider information, tax fraud, and enhancement drugs

Civility

In our day-to-day conduct, we each have the opportunity and obligation to choose how we will conduct ourselves. We might encounter others who are rude, even crude, underhanded, and otherwise not very good conductors of their personal selves in relation to others. It might surprise you to learn that many of the state of Georgia's top leaders, dating back even to heated Civil Rights days, had a way of dealing with one another with civility. It made all the difference in the world. Where other states had major difficulties navigating changes in direction, Georgia was able to build a reputation as a state "too busy to hate." It was often top leaders who met and, whether they agreed or disagreed on issues, did agree that working together in a respectful and civil manner would produce better results—and it did. You have a choice about what you say and how you say it, about creating a divide or extending a hand. When we hear the term "good guys win," this is often what we mean: that those who take the high road generally find each other and are the ones who can make change worth changing for, and in a civil manner. Many of these Georgia leaders—Tom Cousins, Andrew Young, and many others—went on to be named Georgia Trustees. This honor is given by the Georgia Historical Society. The trustees' motto is *Non Sibi, Sed Aliis*, which is Latin for "Not for self but for others."

Get in the Habit

If you form basic bad habits like lying, cheating, and stealing, then doing the right thing will always be a struggle. Get into the habit of being ethical. Even when you think about doing the wrong thing, do the right thing. The next time will be easier, I promise. You will build a reputation as an ethical person plus gain the trust of your employees, customers, and bosses.

You Don't Have to Cheat to Win

How many times have you seen the news—"Bankers Steal Millions!" and "Fraudulent Business!" or "Sexual Harassment Suit Filed"? Oh, Corporate America! Somewhere along the production line, American businesspeople decided to cut corners and do "bad business" to get ahead. You might say, "Sure, business is business. Anything goes, right?"

The Secret's Out

In the last 30 years or so, companies have been cleaning up their acts with ethics! Besides the legal side of things, companies recognized the importance of employee ethics, customer ethics, business ethics, environmental ethics, and any other ethics you can think of. You might argue, "Good guys never win!" but in business, I've discovered that the best guys ALWAYS win. More and more companies are offering ethical training for their employees, and customers are demanding that the products they buy have ethical standards, too.

Wisdom of the Ages

Once, Andrew Young, ambassador to the United Nations, met with the Mohawk Nation. He said, "They told me to respect the wisdom of their ancestors." The Mohawk leaders reminded him that the decisions he made would affect seven generations yet unborn. The Mohawk Indian tribe believed that faith and values and vision could never be just about yourself, but had to be about those who would come after you. This ancient wisdom is a good reminder to us all that ethics is an appreciation for when and how and why things are done. It's important; it matters. And it affects others in the future who will look back with appreciation and respect for those who bothered to make the right decisions.

Who's Got the Ethics? Who's Benefitting?

For the Customer

When you buy a product, you support a business by giving them money. Now, what if that company then gives your money to terrorists? Did you accidentally give money to support terrorist attacks? Or perhaps you discover that your favorite chocolate company buys cocoa from suppliers who use child slave labor? Do you support child slavery?

When you buy a product, it is your responsibility to know what that company believes is RIGHT. You could be indirectly supporting inhumane testing on animals or funding illegal activity. Ethical companies are feeling the pressure to produce ethical products and do the right thing with their revenue. Knowledge is power—do your research, become informed!

For the Employee

It's "finder's keepers" for any employee who lands a position under strong ethical management. An employee ethics policy is like a parent watching out for the children, saying how employees should behave in all situations. Not everybody is polite, ethical, or generally good at interacting with people—in fact, some workplace personalities can be disturbingly rude, mean, bullying, or sexually suggestive.

A strong ethical policy protects employees from other employees and even protects employees from higher management. Bullying, sexual harassment, bribery, favoritism, and racism are all examples of employee problems that you might be involved in. A strong ethical policy can be a guiding light when things get confusing.

For the Employer

Business ethics is good business. Having a sturdy set of ethics can:

- Create a good work environment for all
- Gain customer loyalty
- Improve customer awareness of your brand and business
- Increase revenue. Customers enjoy buying from a company with "good ethics."
- Ensure fair working conditions and compensation for your employees
- Keep your company out of lawsuits!

Ethics is really about being fair to everyone involved. This isn't a perfect world, I know—"life's not fair!" but trying to get as close to "fair" as possible makes for a better business in all respects.

Legally...

Sometimes, companies don't have a choice—the law is the law. Period. Countless laws exist to say what businesses can and cannot do ethically. While it's unethical to discriminate based on anything other than skills, talent and the sheer ability to do a job, it's also illegal. Another example: money laundering is an unethical accounting practice, but it's also illegal. It doesn't matter who you are, whether you're from Miami, Florida or Anchorage, Alaska, a line editor or a heart surgeon, knowing your ethical rights and responsibilities under the law will keep you safe and out of big trouble.

The Ring of Gyges

Once upon a time *there was a shepherd named Gyges from the kingdom of Lydia. One day, as he was tending to his flock, a great storm came out of nowhere. The ground in front of the shepherd split open and his sheep were swallowed into the earth.*

What could the shepherd do but follow his herd? So he went down into the chasm. At the bottom, he found a huge brass horse, hollowed out, with windows on the side. Inside lay the dead body of something which looked like a human, only bigger. The body was naked except for a gold ring on one of the fingers. The shepherd looked around wondering if anyone lived in the pit. Finally, he grabbed the ring, put it on his finger and ran his sheep back up to the land where they grazed.

Gyges and all of the other shepherds in the area met once a month to discuss their flocks. The day after he found the golden ring, he had to go to the next town to one of these meetings. This one was a particularly boring meeting, so he began playing with his ring. The ring had a small green emerald on one side. Well, when the shepherd twisted the stone inside his hand, he became invisible! All of the other shepherds talked about him like he wasn't even there. Then, he twisted the ring back and the others saw him again.

Gyges tested the magic power of the ring several times and decided he could use it to gain fame and fortune. So he planned a way to get to the royal palace by becoming a messenger sent to court. There, Gyges buddied up with the queen and together they plotted to kill the king. With the help of his magic ring, Gyges crept past the palace guards late one night and killed the king in his sleep. Gyges seized the throne and became the most powerful man in the world. No one could outsmart him because of his golden ring.

Some people argue that anyone would turn to crime if they were given the chance to go unpunished. That means that if anyone had a ring like Gyges', that person would start to do bad things no matter how well he or she had behaved before.

Do you think the only reason people don't always break the law is because they are afraid of getting punished? What about an ethical person? Would it be unethical to steal something even if you knew you would never get caught?

Big Ethics Issues

Discrimination

Imagine you run a small stock brokerage. You have five employees—all of them male. You hire a female broker, but you haven't had the time or resources to conduct ethical training for your employees. Two of the men make inappropriate comments to her, and you've heard one verbally explain that she's inferior for being a woman. What do you do?

Would separating men and women into different parts of the office be OK as long as it was "separate but equal?" Is it right to afford special privilege to one sex over the other? How should you teach ethics to your employees?

Discrimination comes in all forms—race, sex, religious, and economic, to name a few of the biggies. You might find yourself in one of the following situations at work. How would you handle it? What is fair, and what is right?

- You are a capable woman who can't seem to move up in the business, and you notice only men command the high-salary positions.
- You are overlooked for promotion to chief mechanic because you are not Caucasian.
- You are a man interviewing for a receptionist position at a country club. You are rejected upon grounds of not suiting the job description. You believe it's because they are looking for a female receptionist.
- You are a female sales agent on a predominantly male team, and you learn that you are paid less for doing the same job.
- You are often teased and harrassed by co-workers about your religious beliefs. What you actually believe is none of their business and it has no affect on how you do your job.
- You are a Muslim-American businesswoman. Every time you pass through Airport Security, the guards search and question you intensively.
- You hear a co-worker making a rude joke about African American stereotypes. You know your friend is offended but won't speak up to defend himself.

What other types of discrimination can you think of? Discuss discrimination on the job first, and then think about other times you might encounter discrimination.

Business Buddies: Partisanship

I have been working as a salesperson on commission for six years now. Two months ago, my boss hired a part-time sales associate. Rather quickly, my boss and the new employee became fast friends, sharing a love of cycling. I have more experience and initiative than the new associate, and I was expecting to get promoted to a newly-created sales team within our company. The off-shoot is this: When it came time for promotion, I was passed over—my boss gave his buddy the job, instead of me.

My boss and I have a strictly professional relationship, and I'm a good worker. What should I do? I had hoped management wouldn't be so partisan.

We've all experienced favoritism, but it still hurts and isn't fair. Is "playing favorites" ever ethical? What if you were the new sales associate? Are you at fault?

Human Resource Question Quandary

In the hiring and interviewing process, employer-to-prospective-employee interaction is confidentially hush-hush. What do you think about this short dilemma scenario:

The music school at a private university is looking to hire a new dean. Mary, the current dean, conducts extensive interviewing and narrows the field to two candidates: Dr. Prine and Dr. Cathy. Both candidates are equally qualified to run the position with only one real difference—Prine is an outside candidate and Cathy is a current faculty member. In the end, Mary offers the job to Prine, who decides to decline the offer for a post at a more prestigious school. Mary then schedules a meeting with Cathy to offer her the position. After Mary makes the proposal, Cathy asks candidly, "Just curious, did you offer the job to the other candidate first?"

Should Mary answer Cathy's question? Or would that be breaking confidentiality? What harm would answering cause, if any? Do you think the answer would affect Cathy's decision to accept the job offer?

On the Side

I'm a Certified Public Accountant (CPA), and I've worked for an accounting firm for ten years. I do my job, of course, but sometimes we have more clients than our firm can handle. The clients like me, so I started managing some accounts independently on the side to make extra money. My boss doesn't know, and I don't plan on telling her, in case there's a problem.

Are my actions unethical? Should I at least inform my boss that I'm taking on extra work? Do I have a responsibility to report those actions to my boss? Do you think I'm breaking my contract?

Proper Pay: Equality?

Federal and state laws require equal pay for equal labor, regardless of race, sex, religion, etc. But, guess what...the problem hasn't gone away! I'm a black woman, and I'll tell you there are still gaping pay differences between men and women, not to mention among white and black and Hispanic workers.

Why do you think this is? If federal laws don't work, what will make pay EQUAL? Can a woman do the same job just as well as a man?

Hard Work: Ethical Employment

Questionable Hiring Practices

I'm the Director of Operations at a small outdoor garden and wedding venue. In addition to managing wedding parties on the garden grounds, I supervise garden maintenance workers. We run a small operation with about six total employees, three of whom are living and working in the U.S. illegally. I know it's against the law to employ these workers, but I feel that it's the ethical thing to do. They are honest and work hard to make a living. Besides, I pay under the table for cheap labor, and I don't have to provide insurance coverage for them. It seems like a win-win situation for everyone.

What do you think? Are illegal immigrants taking jobs from Americans? Are my actions ethical, even though illegal? Are my workers receiving equality as employees? Should they?

Reckless with Responsibility

I'm the head investment broker at a mutual fund company—all the big money from investors goes through me, and I decide which companies to invest in. One Friday, I'm asked to investigate a company's finances for a large client. I'd rather go play golf with some of my buddies from college who are in town. I rush on my research—the company looks solid, I think, so I make the investment quickly and skip out of work early. The next week, my boss asks me, "Why did you invest huge amounts of money in a company headed for bankruptcy?" I don't have a good answer, and I get fired for "gross negligence."

What is negligence? How could I have avoided being negligent? When you take on a job, ask: "What are my responsibilities?"

What other issues do you think might arise in a workplace environment?

Controversy! Questionable Ethics

People argue about what is right and wrong all the time. In the scenarios below, think about both sides of the argument.

Creative Accounting

Maybe you've heard of Occupy Wall Street? People gathered on Wall Street in a protest to hold America's financial wizards accountable for our country's economic problems. After the financial disaster of a company called Enron, many Americans don't trust corporate executives, bankers, and money managers.

Do you think companies should be required to make their financial accounts public knowledge?

Case Study: Enron

The Enron Scandal rocked our nation to its financial core. In a nutshell here's what happened... Enron, an energy company, started having financial losses. The head executives of Enron developed "creative accounting" techniques, which included future predictions of revenue that they hadn't earned. It made the company look FANTASTIC, even though they were still losing money. To hide their losses, Enron created smaller companies (no joke, named after Star Wars characters!) that covered up the trail of lost money. Enron then reported wonderful gains to Wall Street and encouraged the public AND employees to buy stocks. At its peak, stock prices soared to upwards of $90. When a Wall Street reporter released the inside information on Enron's financial woes, the company began crumbling from the inside out. The top executives sold their stock and said "Adios," leaving the company, employees, and shareholders in financial ruin.

Is it important to hold business accounting to ethical standards? Sure, a company has its right to privacy, but shouldn't customers also have a right to know if shady business could cost them LOTS of money? Wouldn't you like to know where all the money goes?

Free Speech Breach: Social Networking

Sitting within the soft glow of your computer screen, furiously typing a blog or tweeting your latest political thoughts, you might forget that clicking "post" means everyone can see it, even your boss. Comments about co-workers and employers are costing employees jobs left and right (political pun not intended) across America. Employers are currently writing rules about what you can and cannot say on social networking sites, even when you're at home. The things you say in the "public" online space is just that—public and available for prying eyes.

Is if fair for employers to restrict your right to free speech online? Where do you stand—is it wrong to talk bad about your co-worker or employer on a social networking site? Or should you be allowed to use free speech whenever, wherever?

We all have the right to free speech, right? I can say whatever I want to say, especially online! YES, you can, but there could be consequences, such as getting canned from a job. Employers are worried that the things you say online could reflect badly on the company. You don't have to look far to find an example of someone fired for using personal opinions to misrepresent the organization or for making derogatory and inappropriate comments about co-workers and employers.

Hey! Where'd You Get That?

When you walk into Wal-Mart, you might forget to ask, "Where does all this stuff come from?" and "How is it so cheap?" Clothing doesn't just magically appear. Imagine this: the cotton comes from India, which is shipped to Taiwan to become cloth, and then sent to factories in the USA to be made into shirts for sale. All the manufacturing parts to the t-shirt puzzle are called the "supply chain." A company can get a really bad reputation if their "supply chains" aren't ethically upstanding.

Case Study: Chocolate Slaves

Who doesn't love a good chocolate bar? Some of the big names in the American candy industry, like Hershey, Nestle, and Ferrero, all bet their reputations on quality cocoa products. Recently, investigations into the supply chains for cocoa discovered some truly disturbing information. Most cocoa comes from suppliers who use children as slaves on the cocoa farms of West African nations like Ghana. These unethical business practices allowed big U.S. companies to purchase cheap cocoa, but at what cost—the price of slavery? After investigations into their supply chains, most major chocolate producers have set a date to end cocoa slavery, some even promising to help create sustainable cocoa farms.

Who is responsible? Are the people who buy and eat chocolate to blame? What about the cocoa farmers themselves—slavery is the only way for them to make a living. Do U.S. chocolate producers have a responsibility to change their suppliers' ethical standards? Why should you care?

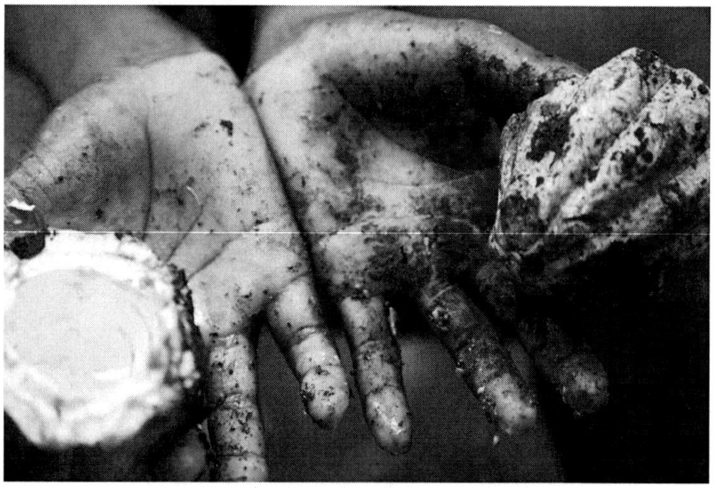

As a consumer, what can you do to stop child slavery?

Environmental Ethics: Not *My* Business

I let toxic pollutants pour into a creek near my business. Does it matter? It's only a little creek and it's on my property. They are not very toxic, just a little toxic. There is no law at this time to keep me from doing this. No one sees me because the creek is in some woods. I'm not going to do it forever, just 20 or 30 years until I retire. I give a lot of people jobs and that helps a lot of families around here. Besides, it would cost me a bundle to get rid of the toxic pollutants in any other way.

What do you think?

Adam: *I think this is ok. I live here and I sure don't want to lose my job. I have six kids, you know. Besides, I live down the creek and the water seems ok to me. We swim in it and eat fish we catch from it all the time.*

Emily: *This is terrible! These toxins are very dangerous. They can cause cancer. Even though everything seems ok now, it won't in 10 or 12 years when people start getting sick.*

Raul: *Nobody better complain about what this company is doing, even if it is polluting the water. We need their tax money. If they were to get mad at this community and move somewhere else, we'd all be out of work.*

Juanita: *I know what that plant is doing and it hurts me. I live 20 miles down the creek and it's killing all the fish in my part of the creek. So, even though those people at the plant don't lose their jobs, I am losing mine because I can't make a living here on the creek fishing anymore. I am going to have to move away. How fair is that?*

What is right and what is wrong? What is ethical when no one is breaking any law? When no one knows what's going on? When people will be hurt if you do something different anyway?

Don't be surprised if your business, or one you work for, has to handle hot issues like global warming, toxic pollution, and resource management. Think about where you stand on these issues.

Today's Ethical Issues

A lot of people think ethical considerations are more complicated today than they used to be. What do you think? Do you think this means that they will be even more complicated when you are an adult? Even if they are more complicated, should that be an excuse to lie? Cheat? Steal? What should it be an excuse to do?

If modern days and technology have made it harder to be ethical, what should we do about it? What is the problem? Who should solve it? Why?

Here are just a few contemporary ethical considerations, things that perhaps our grandparents didn't have to worry about. See if you think it makes any difference. Can you think of a comparison to any of the following problems—even back in the Dark Ages, Caveman Days, the Victorian Era, or the Old West?

The U. S. Patent Office has decided to allow inventors to patent new forms of animal life! Modern science has given us the ability to change life. There are many ways this new technology can be used. It can be used for good, such as to produce a healthier animal or a virus that can save lives. But it can be used for bad purposes, such as to abuse forms of life or to make new forms of animals that could harm us.

What ethical questions does this bring up? If we are allowed to create new kinds of animals, should we be allowed to create new forms of human beings, too?

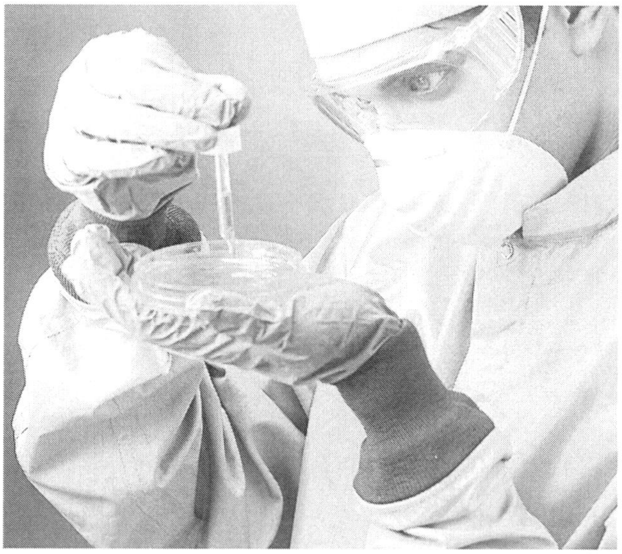

Sports and ethics have been in the news a lot. Discuss your feelings about the following ethical considerations:

-Is it ok to pay a high school student to come to your college because he is the best quarterback you've ever seen and you really want him on your team?

-Isn't it all right to pass a college student on to the next grade, even if he is failing, when he would be kicked off the team if he didn't pass?

-If NO DRUGS is the rule on the team, and the best player breaks the rule, isn't it best not to punish him since it would punish the whole team if he doesn't play?

It has come out that law officers have staged fake drug raids. They do not even tell the police who will conduct the raid that the drugs have been planted there ahead of time and that the bust is not for real. Reporters come to the drug bust and think it is a real one and write about it in their newspapers, which we read and believe. Drug enforcement officials say these false drug busts help them keep drugs off the streets. Everyone wants that, don't they? Is doing it this way unethical or not?

No matter which way you decide, what could such a practice lead to? Is this worth worrying about?

Three companies are going to bid on a million-dollar job. While every company really wants the job, the two largest companies decide to compare the price they will bid. They agree that one of them will bid low and get the job, and then next time, it will bid high so the other company can get the job. The third company does not know anything about this plan. Besides, it is smaller and probably won't bid really low anyway. When the sealed bids are opened, sure enough, the big company gets the job.

Was this ethical? Legal?

Discuss what "bid rigging" and "collusion" mean. Why aren't the two companies playing fair under the "free enterprise" system?

Tech Troubles

Lots of kids have computers. Software is expensive so many young adults are downloading copies online through "peer-to-peer" (P2P) sharing programs. And not just software… music, movies, books, and TV shows too! It's easy to do, and free!

Is this OK? Who loses money? What is a copyright law?

If you grow up to become a software maker, how will it change your mind about downloading free software? Do kids know that what they're doing is stealing? If not, why don't they know? If they do know, do they still do it? Why or why not?

Facebook usually ends up being Gossipbook, but when does gossip become cyber-bullying? Imagine Emily posts this comment about the "new girl," Margret who just moved to town: "I can't stand her. The world would be better off without her." Several other people follow up with "LOL" and "Yeah, she's so weird. Did you see her clothes?"

If said in person, would these comments be considered bullying? Does saying it online make it OK, or is it cyber-bullying? People say whatever they want on social networking sites, so what harm can a little gossip do?

What other modern-day ethical questions can you think of?

Coffee or the Cup: Which Do You Prefer?

There's an old parable, a wise story if you will, about coffee that goes like this:

A group of high school graduates went back to see their most beloved teacher. As the students griped and complained about this or that, stress and money, and the difficulties of work life, the teacher put out several cups—porcelain, glass, crystal, plastic, some expensive looking, and others plain tin. Then the teacher asked, "Does anyone care for coffee?"

Smelling the freshly brewed coffee, the graduates gladly accepted, chose cups, and helped themselves to the coffee.

"I couldn't help but notice," the teacher said, "that all of the nice-looking and expensive cups have been snatched up. It is only natural for you to want the best for yourselves—but that is the source of your problems and stress.

"Believe me, the cup itself adds no quality to the coffee," he said. "In most cases, it is more expensive and even hides what we drink. What you really desired was the coffee, not the cup, but you consciously went for the cups, and then you even began eyeing each other's cups.

"Now consider this: Your Life is the coffee; your job, money, and position in society are the cup. They are just tools to hold and contain Life, and the type of cup we have does not define, nor change the quality of life we live.

"Sometimes, by concentrating only on the cup, we fail to enjoy the coffee.

"So, I say to you… savor the flavor and drink up."

But What About Ethics?

What do coffee and cups have to do with ethics?? It's all connected, I promise, in more ways than one. It's easy to lose sight of what is important, especially in the business world. Being an average-Joe or Jane employee, freewheeling business owner, or slick corporate executive comes with responsibilities. Littered with temptations, pitfalls, and ethical dilemmas, business situations can get sticky–will you be tempted by high profits, or perhaps lose your cool when that pesky co-worker "borrows" your tools? We're only human, and without a reminder, we all will, somewhere along that long line, fail to remember that sturdy ethical practices are what make you, your boss, and your company strong both inside and out.

Economic Stewardship

Can you guess what all these people have in common?

- *•Microsoft Corporation founder and philanthropist Bill Gates*
- *•Former President Jimmy Carter*
- *•Businessman and philanthropist Ted Turner*
- *•Baseball legend Hank Aaron*
- *•Home Depot co-founder Bernie Marcus*
- *•TV mogul Oprah Winfrey*
- *•Dr. Martin Luther King, Jr., Civil Rights leader and Nobel Prize winner*
- *•Tom Cousins, developer and philanthropist*
- *•Andrew Young, Civil Rights leader and former U.N. Ambassador*
- *•Business magnate, investor and philanthropist Warren Buffett*
- *•Robert Woodruff, head of Coca-Cola*
- *•Gregg Steinhafel, CEO of Target*
- *•Truett Cathy, Chick-fil-A founder*
- *•Walmart founder Sam Walton*

They are all real life examples of successful and ethically upstanding individuals who valued *economic stewardship.* What is economic stewardship? I'm glad you asked. It's the idea that money and service should be invested wisely to support community and business growth. What good is money and talent if you just blow it on yourself? Think of Ebenezer Scrooge—he had all the money in the world, but he wasn't happy.

To be a steward means you take care of something. An economic steward uses his/her money wisely to take care of the public, often through charities, education programs, civil rights agendas, or by investing in small businesses to help grow the community.

Part of your responsibility as an adult is to decide what role you want to play. Doing something truly useful with your time, money, and resources will bring great joy to your life. Life fulfillment can't be measured, but when all is said and done, what will your legacy be?

Exercises in Ethics

Here are some examples of the kinds of ethical situations people encounter. See what action you would take or decision you would make. Discuss why you chose that way. What would someone else possibly choose? What would their decision mean?

By the way, many of these examples were taken from newspaper headlines, so these are real choices people have had to make. Some people act ethically. Some don't and often end up fired, in jail, or in big trouble. Some people don't seem to get in trouble at all, but they sure cause other people a lot of it!

1. You are a farmer. To grow your crops, you must use a lot of chemical fertilizers to keep bugs from destroying the crops before they are harvested. The rain washes these chemicals off your land and into nearby creeks and rivers. The chemicals in the runoff kill the fish. The people who fish for a living complain that you are running them out of business. There are ways to grow crops with less fertilizer, but it is harder and may mean your crop is smaller. *What do you do?*

2. You are the chief production engineer for a large automobile manufacturer. You have started final production of the newest model. A safety inspector brings a slight problem to your attention—the braking mechanism on a few out of every 10,000 vehicles has defective parts. It is impossible to identify which of the new cars have "issues." Do you put the new model on the market? Or do you stop the whole production until the issue is fixed? One way could cost lives, but the other would possibly cost you your job. *How would you handle it?*

3. The space shuttle is all prepared to take off. The weather is a little colder than everyone had planned on. In fact, there is ice on part of the ship that is not really supposed to get too cold. You are just a worker on the launch. Do you let someone know that you think the launch should be postponed or do you just do your job—after all, that's someone else's decision to make.

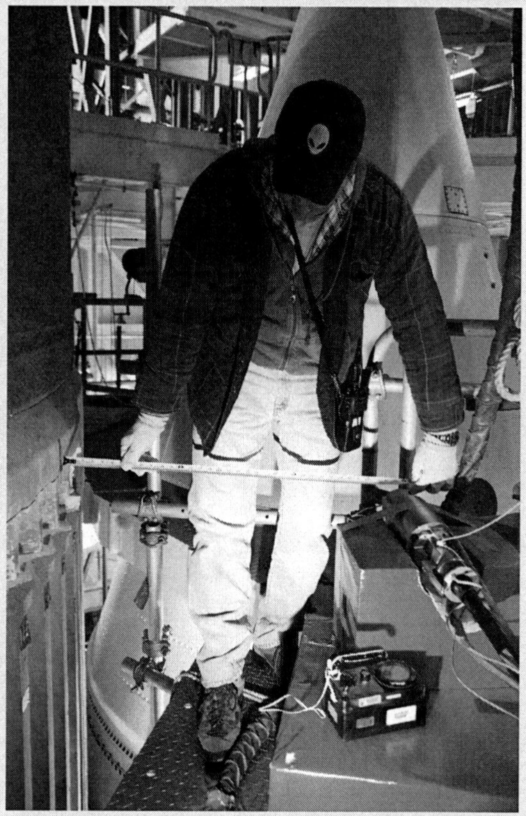

You decide to report the ice to your boss and recommend that the launch be postponed.

Next, your boss talks with others about postponing the mission. This is not something the big boss is going to like to hear. Everyone agrees that it is getting warmer every minute. Even the worker who reported the possible problem said that. Everyone decides just to go on, especially since it is almost launch time. But you really believe that the big boss should be notified. *What do you do?*

You talk the others into telling the big boss. He is very upset. Everything else is in perfect order. Why is everyone worried about a little ice?! Surely all this has been checked out before. The decision is made for the launch to go on—since everyone and everything is ready. The likelihood of the cold weather really being a problem is a million to one.

Was this a good decision? Why or why not?

Now, go back in time...Many months before, another worker worries about the effect of cold weather on this part of the shuttle. He thinks it could really cause a problem sometime in the future. Now seems to be the best time to take care of it. This is what he tells his boss. But his boss disagrees. Money is tight. Time is short. He doesn't need any new problems; he's got enough problems as it is. So things go on as they are. But it bothers the worker enough that he goes over his boss's head and tells someone else. The worker ends up getting fired for this. Or is it for this? Most people do not think it is ethical to go over your boss's head. But are there any exceptions? Is he fired because he did this? Or is he let go because too many people are afraid that the worker will keep bothering everyone about this problem which will just take a lot of time and cost everyone a lot of money?

What do you think? When you relate this earlier ethical incident to the later one, who was really at fault?

Discuss small ethical decisions versus big ones. When are small decisions not small at all? What if the shuttle had taken off without any mishap—would that have meant the worker was wrong? Would it have meant that the earlier worker was wrong?

4. You are about to graduate from a major military school. This school has always had a strict honor code. Lying is not tolerated. However, you are caught lying, so according to the rules that everyone else has abided by, you are dismissed from the school. But you have some political friends who intervene and manage to get you put back in school. Your fellow classmates are shocked. You are relieved. *Did this situation turn out right? Why or why not?*

Is it ever OK to tell a "little white lie?" Example: You've had a terrible day. A co-worker says, "Hey! How are you?" Do you say, "I'm fine, thanks," or do you tell her all about your terrible day?

5. You buy this book from me. You like it so much that you want to send your friend a copy. But instead of buying another copy, you just copy the pages of this one on a copier and send it to her. *Is this against the law? Is it ethical? Is it ethical only if you don't get caught?*

People who make unethical decisions often do get caught in the trap they have set for themselves. If there is a law against the action they have taken, then they can be punished by being charged a fine or going to jail.

If there is not a real law, but there is some code of ethics everyone has agreed to go by, then they may be reprimanded (called on the carpet) by their colleagues. This may just embarrass them or perhaps remind them of what they agreed to. It may make them so angry they drop out of the group. Or the group may insist they drop out. Perhaps you have seen some of these types of situations in Congress recently. Congressmen are called before the Ethics Committee to explain some deed that seems to go against the agreements everyone has made. If they cannot show a good reason for their actions, then they may be asked to resign. They could even be charged with a crime if their unethical conduct was also against the law.

Think about these questions:

Why are people ethical?

Are we only ethical when we are forced to be so?

Who is the most ethical person you know? Is he only that way because there are rules or laws? If there were no rules or laws, how do you think that person would act? Why?

If you were going to write one rule of ethics to govern your actions, what would it be?

Write Your Own Code of Ethics

It can be plain, simple, long, or short. You can change it whenever you want to. Make a copy to keep on your dresser or in your pocket. When you have ethical decisions to make, remind yourself—by looking at this list—of the kind of person you want to be.

Here are some examples:

One man wrote a book called *All I Really Need to Know I Learned in Kindergarten*. Some of the things he listed included:

"Share everything. Play fair. Don't hit people. Put things back where you found them. Clean up your own mess. Don't take things that aren't yours. Say you're sorry when you hurt somebody."

I'm sure you'll find resources for inspiration that mean even more to you. Here are some thoughts that one kid gave to me. Some really bad stuff had happened to this kid. I won't tell you what—just pretend it was something you'd hate to have happen to you. "How did you get through this bad stuff?" I asked. The kid, about your age, gave me her own list of ethics that she had created just for herself. It goes something like this:

In your own judgment, do the best you can.
Accept full responsibility for your own actions.
Take care of practical things first.
Maintain your own domain.
Have the best health possible.
Replace bad habits with good ones.
Don't worry about what "won't matter in a hundred years."
Get up and stay up.
Improve all your human relations.
Create your own version of beautiful.

And, lastly, here are some ethics I made up for a person I just finished reading about. I don't know if this was his code of ethics, but see what you think:

- *Even though I am poor and live in a log cabin, I will teach myself the things I need to know to live a good and helpful life.*

- *Even though I will run a grocery store that fails and puts me in deep debt, I will not lie or cheat or steal to solve my problems.*

- *Even though I may run for the Senate twice and lose both times, I will not give up on my faith to achieve my destiny.*

- *Even though I eventually hold the most powerful post in my nation, I will not abuse the power but use it for the betterment of man.*

- *Even though what I must do to live a moral and ethical life may bring me death, I will be brave enough to always live up to the standards I set for myself.*

This man, the man who freed the slaves, did die for what he believed in. But Abraham Lincoln set ethical standards that are still worth living by today. And somehow, you feel that no matter how many seemingly good excuses he might have been offered: "life's too hard, things are too complicated, or the technology is too far advanced"—that it would not have deterred him from being "Honest Abe" in all aspects of his life, simple or complex, today...yesterday...or tomorrow.

How about you?

ETIQUETTE means behaving yourself a little better than is absolutely essential

—Will Cuppy, humorist

Section 2: ETIQUETTE

What Is Etiquette?

The rules of etiquette are taken directly from ethical rules like being kind, courteous, and polite—you know... "doing unto others." In fact, some business-minded people think that doing business by the "Golden Rule" is the best way to run a company, not just for peace of mind—but it is also the best way to make money, too!

I'll bet you think etiquette is a long laundry list of "dos and don'ts." It might seem that way if you don't already have the basics of courtesy and consideration toward others. Etiquette is a **positive** thing, a way of being that benefits yourself and your co-workers. We're talking about kindergarten lessons like sharing supplies and saying "please" and "thank you," which lead us to better things like respect, civility and a positive work environment. Etiquette, in a nutshell, is being considerate and fair, to yourself and others.

So, please, be considerate, and thank you for listening.

Civil Service

No matter what your peers in school or work do, it's crucial to err on the side of being civil. No one welcomes a bully, or those who make petty comments, or are rude, abrasive or screaming, backbiting, or have any other "I'm the center of the universe" attitude at work.

Everyone is busy and stressed, on deadline, had a flat tire, or an argument with their mother...but there is no excuse for not being civil. Add "please" to anything you ask for; say "thanks" when someone assists you, no manner how minor the duty. Apologize when it's needed.

You might think being rude and crude makes you seem cool, but instead you come across as uncouth and ill-mannered. Respect people, whether they are higher on the job ladder than you are, or lower. Be professional with everyone.

What happens when you act badly? It reflects poorly on you and your company or department. It drains productivity because everyone has to stop and talk about the "situation." It affects company loyalty, and customers really don't appreciate seeing the people they are doing business with acting badly.

Of course you won't agree with everyone, nor they with you. Naturally, you will get irritated from time to time, or aggravated, or even angry. But you're not a kid anymore, not in the eyes of the workplace.

Here are a few things to practice:

- Use good manners all the time; set the tone no matter how others behave.
- Be polite.
- Show respect.
- Don't respond to uncivil co-workers with incivility, that just escalates things.
- Self-monitor your behavior; don't wait to get called-out about it—how embarrassing!
- Watch for triggers that push your buttons; work extra hard not to respond negatively, since you know those things will happen from time to time. Defuse your own bomb!
- Learn to handle conflict. Conflict is natural in the work world; if you are not sure how to do this, ask your supervisor for tips on how to express yourself or react in an acceptable manner.
- Watch for emails or text messages that can too easily come across as snide.
- Dress appropriately, be on time, and smile—co-workers are more apt to work well with you if you look like you mean good business.
- Remember that good etiquette is not a sign of weakness, it's a sign of good up-bringing, even if you brought yourself up!
- Accept responsibility for your actions and the consequences; learn from your mistakes or missteps.
- Ask for feedback on your behavior...you'll get it!

Your Boss Is Your Customer...

Did you ever think of it that way? *Your boss is your client. How you treat your client/customer (perhaps especially your bo*ss!) can affect your future tremendously. As a long-time freelance writer, I always felt that my customer was my boss, so it works either way. I tried to treat my clients as if I worked for them—because I did while I was on their project.

Have you ever experienced bad service when you were a customer? Yeah, I know...sometimes five times a day! Often people forget who is the customer and who is the boss, so to speak. This very day, I was in a home improvement store and was told, "No, the manager of the electrical department can't come out and help you...he's in a management meeting with his boss."

Management Rule No. 1: The customer is the boss! If this man's boss was a good manager, he would certainly rush the electrical manager out of the meeting to help the customer, the real boss! Confused?

It's not confusing at all; knowing who is who is essential.
Sometimes, it doesn't seem very clear. If you go to see your principal, you might feel like she's the boss, but she works for you! If you go to a banker for a loan, he or she is not the customer—you are—you will be paying them money back, plus interest. Think about all this and keep it straight in your head.

If your boss is your customer:

- Be just as courteous and respectful and helpful as you would to a "real" customer.
- Be of great assistance and put his needs, schedule, and deadlines ahead of your own.
- Anticipate her needs and requirements.
- And always say, "Thank you" when you receive your paycheck.

A boss who is treated like your customer:

- Is loyal; you have looked out for them and they will look out for you.
- Reciprocates; she will be so appreciative of your attitude that she will bend over backwards to try to help you as well.
- Will develop admiration for you, both as an employee and a person.
- And when the time comes to consider who should replace them as they move up the company ladder, will certainly consider you...and should you choose to work elsewhere, be the first to highly recommend you.

You could say this is a Big Deal. It's how long-term professional and powerful relationships are born. If your boss (or former boss) starts his or her own business, guess who'll be called first? It's more than goodwill and good etiquette, it's a good investment.

You are MY customer, and I appreciate you very much!

Speech! Speech!

"Speech is the mirror of the soul; as a man speaks, so he is." — Publilious Syrus

The words coming out of your mouth are the most telling part of your personality. Someone once said, "Be careful when you speak, because you might say something you haven't thought of." Speaking professionally is a bit of an art. Think before you speak until business practice makes you speak business perfect.

To speak with proper business etiquette doesn't require a prim and proper British accent or flowery perfume on your breath. The basics of politeness, grammar, and clarity will do.

Speaking Politely

An employer assumes that if you can't do the small things right, like being polite, the bigger aspects of your work life will suffer as well. Social niceties are, well...NICE. You'll hear me harp on saying "please" and "thank you." I don't care if you're a hotshot boss with legions of loyal employees. When asking an employee to do something, it's important to ask politely—employees are people, too, and deserve respect.

On the customer's end, nobody in his or her right mind would pay for disrespectful service. The politeness and courtesy of your employees is directly related to your customer's satisfaction and your business! Remember, the boss is the customer and the customer is the boss.

Slowly and Clearly

Do you know anyone who talks a million words a minute? Or how about someone who mumbles? I find myself saying "Huh?" "What did you say?" and "Could you repeat that?" Our normal speech, day in and day out, is riddled with laziness, from dropping endings (I'm goin' huntin') to combining words (I'm gonnago hunting) and stringing together sentences so long you could get lost—or lose somebody else! In an interview scenario, speaking slowly and enunciating your vowels and consonants paves the road to an even-paced, clear-as-a-bell conversation that is focused on YOU and your skills. I'm 100 percent certain you have important things to say, so don't just be heard—be understood.

Grammar Groans

I've met brilliant people who had terrible grammar and people smarter than me who had worse spelling. It is particularly important to use correct grammar when meeting a new employer or business contact. Speaking grammatically can make a great first impression by showing that you are educated and care about speaking correctly.

Yeah, I break grammar rules sometimes…but the difference is, I know grammar, and choose when, and when not, to break the rules! You can't always speak in purely grammatical sentences—humans don't do that—but the better your grammar, the more educated you look to an employer.

Here are some grammar items to clean up before you head into that first job interview:

- "Ain't" is a word, but it ain't got any place in work etiquette.
- Don't not watch your double negatives.
- "I've got" is one I'm guilty of saying. For example, "I've got a problem," instead of "I have a problem." Try to eliminate "got" as much as possible, unless you actually "got" something… "I got a raise!"
- Avoid starting sentences with "There's" and "Here's" because it can lead to subject-verb agreement problems later on. For instance, I might naturally start a sentence "There's many people who don't have good grammar." Grammatically, it should be "There ARE many people…"
- "Like, you know, the best, like, friend ever." Don't sell yourself short by using "like" like this.
- Even if you ramble, try to avoid run-on sentences that never end. Consolidate your thoughts into straightforward, direct speech.
- A common usage error is "your" and "you're." When I get into an email typing frenzy, my "your" becomes "you're,"—even a seasoned grammar veteran like myself has slip-ups. Another common usage error is "there," "their," and "they're." Be careful!

But It Was Just a Colorful Joke!

"Have you heard this one? It goes...a red dog, a blue dog and a green dog go into a store. The red one says..."

Is *that* type of joke OK in the office, or even a warehouse? What about "blonde" jokes? Or hey! What about that funny one about short people? Let's have a serious chat here for a moment. The key to good work etiquette is making sure people have comfortable relationships. Work is a place where everyone should feel comfortable, unthreatened, and valued.

Jokes about race, sex, and gender can be REALLY funny, but are based on stereotypes that just aren't true. In fact, those jokes, however you mean to say them, are offensive! They hurt feelings, and just because you think they're hilarious doesn't mean they won't make someone else feel bad. Leave the jokes to the professionals—comedians need work, too.

Whatever your views on these sensitive issues, it's in your best professional interest to keep racist, sexist, homophobic, political, or religious comments and jokes at home.
It's really as simple as "If you can't say anything nice, don't say anything at all." Would you look at that, we're back to kindergarten rules again! I told you etiquette is easy.

Another Mouth Disease: SWEARING

In a recent article by Susan Ricker, she reports that survey data indicate 51 percent of workers swear on the job. On the other hand, 81 percent of employers said that swearing brings one's professionalism into question, and 57 percent of employers said they would be less likely to promote a person who curses at work. Could using "bad words" come between you and a promotion? Here's a good four-letter word: DON'T.

Dress the Part

When it comes to dressing the professional part, you'll find yourself asking… "*What should I wear? Do I show off my one-of-a-kind fashion flair, or should I conform to what everyone else is wearing? Is this cute enough—or maybe TOO cute? I'm not concerned with appearance, so why is my boss stuck up? I thought I left dress codes behind in middle school. What's the big deal about business casual anyway?*"

Just to get your brain firing in all fashions, think about which one of these applicants you would hire for the position of supervisor at your firm. Assume that all applicants are qualified (on paper) for the position, and asked to meet for a one-on-one interview.

• A woman dressed in a green three-piece twill suit with a cutesy, pink bow tie at her neck—solid green pumps on her feet.

• A man wearing full suit and tie. His hair looks ungroomed, but otherwise he is well put together and carrying a briefcase with portfolio items and documentation.

• A man in washed-out jeans and a "straight from the beach" look with faded Hawaiian shirt and sandals. His resume looks fabulous, but he's not wearing a belt, and his pants are sagging and dragging.

• A woman who wears a knee-length black skirt, white blouse, and cardigan. She comes well-prepared with briefcase and all accompanying documents

• A man with a collared shirt, dress pants, and black loafers. He tells you he forgot his tie at home, and you notice that his fly is unzipped. (Oops!)

• A woman wearing a mid-thigh silk dress with straps exposing most of her shoulders. Halfway through the interview she pulls out a sweater and covers up her shoulders.

Confused? I'll give you some inside information. Professional dress code will make or break you.

If you don't remember anything else, remember this: **What you wear depends on where you work.** Dress according to the general atmosphere of wherever you work. A beach bum might have the proper dress to work at a surf shop. In most professions, specific attire is standard. You will need to dress similarly to others by observing standards of "decency" according to the type of work. The most rigorous and conservative is, of course, the business world of lawyers, executives, bankers, stock brokers, etc.

The most successful people always seem to find the right fit when it comes to attire. I prefer, like most people, to wear "business casual."

Business Casual: Best described as that "clean" look. When dressing business casual, you should feel comfortable, but also look sharp and put together. Companies adopt a business casual dress code to give employees comfort while maintaining a professional image for customers, business associates, and community visitors. For men, the essentials are slacks and a button-up, collared shirt.

Remember, business casual isn't business shabby-don't-give-a-hoot. There is such a thing as TOO casual.

For women, the options are more varied. Many women choose fairly conservative skirts, blouses and tops. Others prefer a tailored suit or the softer appearance of a dress.

Interview Etiquette

There are whole books written to prepare you for an interview. This isn't one of them. We understand that interviewing well takes practice and experience. The best way to get into the professional groove is to take a crack at it, hit it with all you have, and learn from your mistakes. That being said, there are some major etiquette blunders you can avoid whether it's your first or last interview.

- **Dress appropriately.** Remember, your dress should immediately make your interviewer think, "Wow, we need her/him on our team!" For an interview, business casual is usually acceptable, unless you are interviewing for a high professional position such as doctor or lawyer, for which formal dress attire is suggested.
- **Be on time.** "On time" means a few minutes early, not fashionably late. In fact, there's no such thing as "fashionably" late in the business world. If you're late, it's rude, not a matter of style.
- **Demeanor:** Your *professional* demeanor says everything about you as an employee. Walk in levelheaded, ready to do, say, and act your best. Remember to be courteous and polite.
- **Introduce yourself and sit down when asked.**
- **Making small talk** about the weather or current events can be helpful to break the tension, but stay far, far, far away from controversial topics.
- **Don't put documents on the interviewer's desk.** Try to be respectful of another person's turf. If you have portfolio material to present, ask if you can use the desk space before setting anything down.
- **Closing:** Your interviewer will typically recap the things you've discussed and then stand to say farewell. Shake hands if offered.
- **The very next day, send a thank you note.** Trust me, this one pays off!

Body Language: When You Say Nothing at All

Being quiet doesn't make you a closed book—if you're not revealing of your content, then people will judge you by your cover. The way you act on the outside is just as important as the things you say. The gestures you make, the way you stand, the eye contact you give, all speak volumes about your confidence, your professional etiquette, and your character as an employee.

Posture

When you look in the mirror and relax, do you slouch down? I bent over a school desk for years (fell asleep on them, too!), and I've been in a posture war with myself ever since. Whether or not you're a confident person, stand up straight and dare to be professional.

Now, I'm not asking you to attach a 2x4 plank to your back all the time, but having good posture is beneficial in professional encounters such as interviews, board meetings, or presentations. Stand-up-straight-and-proud posture asserts confidence and commands presence in a room. Try to straighten up when you need to, pull your shoulders back, and keep your head up—you have reason to be proud.

Eye Contact

Eyes are often called the windows to the soul, so be aware of what you do with them. Think about some of your habits. Do you blink a lot when you're nervous? When speaking, do you look at other things in the room, or look up when you're thinking? Do you tend to look away when you lose interest? Are you so afraid of breaking eye contact that you bore holes into another person's skull?

Good eye contact (solid and confident, but not too intense) establishes trust as well as demonstrates confidence and respect for what another person is saying. It's OK to break eye contact while speaking, I promise, but always bring your focus back to the other person.

Facial Expressions

If you're nervous, scared, anxious, tired, or angry, your face will show it, and that's OK. For an interview, practice relaxing your face, get into your Zen zone, and un-furrow that brow. A confident smile and a well-timed laugh can really put you and your interviewer at ease!

An Etiquette Note: Arms and Legs

Arms and legs can also be a body-talking point—shuffling your feet or constantly fidgeting can indicate nervousness or restlessness. Folding your arms can indicate a closed attitude that says you're not ready to listen or speak. Try to open yourself up. Remember not to put your elbows on the interview table, and avoid touching your face too much or resting your head on your hands. "Am I boring you?" the interviewer may wonder.

The best advice is to remain relaxed. Figure out what is comfortable for you—remember where your arms and legs feel most natural, and let the employer see YOU, not your fear of blowing it—and you won't!

Demeanor: Professionalism

What the heck is *demeanor*? Honestly, it's hard to define, and even harder to say what qualities make up a "good demeanor," but hey, I'm a professional and giving up is not in my job description!

Webster's dictionary defines demeanor as *your behavior toward others.* It is the way you speak, act, dress, and generally present yourself to other people. Are you rude, offensive, or overbearing? You might have a quiet or somber demeanor, or perhaps you're the bubbly, happy-go-lucky type. In any business situation, regardless of your personality, you want to carry yourself with the best "professional demeanor." All that means is looking, speaking, and acting professional. A professional always arrives on time, keeps confidential info confidential, uses clean, professional language, and refrains from spewing personal opinions about clients or co-workers. Easy, right? Let's take a look...

It's amazing how much of hiring and firing has to do with demeanor. Of course, skills and qualification get your foot in the interview room, but finding the right professional fit is at least half the battle, if not most of the war. There's not one rule I can give you—a professional demeanor requires a lot of different things rolled together into one polished professional. First, last, and in between, a professional demeanor requires courtesy.

Courtesy

It makes the professional world go round. Think about it a minute: who wants to work for someone who is offensive, inconsiderate, and generally disrespectful? I'll bet top dollar you wouldn't hire someone who showed blatant disregard for you and your company.

I'm not going to list a thousand things you need to remember, because the "Golden Rule" covers almost all other ethical and etiquette considerations. The rules of etiquette have their origins in morality, ethics, and even religion, so it makes sense to live by the maxim, "Do unto others as you would have them do unto you."

If it seems like a nice gesture, or the *right* thing to do, DO IT (please)! Hold a door for someone, ask before taking, say "you're welcome" instead of "no problem," acknowledge the hard work of your peers, and treat others with the respect they deserve. A personable personality will pay off. The business world isn't so much "dog eat dog" as it is about building profitable relationships.

Just the Right Fit

Beyond being courteous, employers are looking for a skilled, valuable, enthusiastic member to join their team. When I say "valuable," I mean having the invisible qualities that make a great workplace professional: the essence of good character, a positive can-do attitude, and the willingness to get the details right—skills that are almost impossible to teach.

Looking flawless on a resume won't automatically win you a position. An employer desperately wants someone who is a great team player, who believes in the company's vision, and who has the professional demeanor to properly represent their business.

There's a fine, invisible line between employees who are active and valuable within a company and those who do the bare minimum to get the job done. Plenty of people will meet the qualifications for your position, but by being just the right fit, and being "valuable," you can ensure your skills are irreplaceable!

Mixed Messages

Have you ever said one thing but meant something else, or your actions weren't true to your words? What we say and hear, do and see, are often far from what was meant. "Mixed messages" come in all different packages—physical, verbal, personal, and professional. Take a personal relationship, for example: You make a new friend. One day she compliments your clothes and makes plans with you to hang out on the weekend. The next day she ignores you—that's called a mixed message. Think about these specific scenarios and consider what kind of mixed messages you want to avoid sending, and receiving, in a business situation.

This is a simple one. Your boss or supervisor asks you to clean up your workspace (just like your mom!). You slouch back and roll your eyes, saying "Yes, Ma'am," or "Okaaay, sir." *What did you REALLY say?*

Imagine a Public Relations department for a large corporation has consistently branded their products as family-friendly. BUT, on a new assignment, the marketing department starts pushing the envelope with sex appeal to "spice-up" their advertising campaign. *How should management address these mixed messages sent to the public?*

The department head hands you an assignment and says, "Take your time, I want quality work," but the project manager is rushing you to stay on schedule. *What do you do when receiving mixed signals from two different authorities?*

Usually, your co-worker is a complete jerk to you, makes snide comments, and talks about you behind your back. One week, he invites you for a Friday get-together with some co-workers. You have conflicted feelings about accepting. *What do you do?*

Sending the Right Signals

Stop sending unintentional mixed messages and avoid unprofessional mix-ups.

1. **Walk the talk.** If at all possible, put your actions in line with your words. That means, instead of rolling your eyes and saying "yes, sir," have a discussion with your boss about misgivings or problems with management, or maybe it's as easy as cleaning your desk!

2. **Avoid making others uncomfortable** by refraining from inappropriate touching, crude comments, jokes, or racial and sexist remarks. To avoid serious conflict and confrontation, religion and politics are usually taboo subjects in the workplace. Also, don't stand too close to someone. As a general rule, men tend to need less personal space than women—guys, keep that in mind!

3. **Be clear about how you feel.** If you like someone, make it known to him or her. If you want things to be purely platonic, professional, and friendly, establish those boundaries from the start. Nipping any unwanted relationships in the bud early can avoid mixed emotions and conflict situations later on.

4. **Make sure the things you do and say publicly and professionally reflect the ethical values of the company or organization.** Simply—don't say anything you wouldn't write and sign.

5. **Limit sarcasm...**OK, pin the tail on me. I'm the donkey. I'm a sharp, snarky, sarcastic employer, but what if someone misunderstands my sarcasm? To be funny, I often say one thing but mean another, and if misunderstood, sarcasm gives confusing, mixed signals. I'm sure to be very clear first, and then try my luck with wit.

Confidentiality

**"Can I tell you a secret? **I'm confident you won't tell a soul."

Confidentiality is an agreement between a client and a professional that any information discussed will not be offered or sold to any other party. It is not only a good idea, it's often an ethical law.

Living in the information age is great! I love having the world at the click of a Google search—it seems like we're all information surfers these days. In the business world, companies are benefiting, too, by creating databases full of consumer information for target advertising by region and population. There are also plentiful background checks and access to employer information. Now, what does all that have to do with confidentiality?

Reasons for Confidentiality

Do you really want anyone, anywhere, having access to your private information? I assume you're not hiding skeletons in the closet. Are you? (Oh, wait, you don't have to tell me, but if you do, I'll keep it confidential.)

Most professionals agree to a legal confidentiality agreement—as they should. This type of business confidentiality protects your personal information such as bank accounts, legal documentation, social security, and credit card numbers. With new forms of information hacking, stolen identity is on the rise, so be careful whom you give information to. You wouldn't hand over your life to just anybody you meet on the street!

Employers have direct access to your most private information, such as your financial records, work history, as well as any criminal record found in a background check. Employers have a responsibility to keep all information about their employees under lock and key away from prying eyes.

Professional fields where client confidentiality is a key feature:

- Lawyer-to-client confidentiality to ensure trust
- Medical confidentiality between doctors and patients
- Therapist-to-client confidentiality to ensure safety of *personal* information

Confidentiality is usually held between these main groups:

- Employer to Employee
- Company to Consumers
- Professional to Client

Name of the Game

Workplace etiquette doesn't get more fundamental or important than learning, remembering, and using names. *"Beth...Bertha...Beatrice...I'm sorry. What was your name?"* Remembering a name immediately establishes a personal connection—customers love it, employers require it. Even in emails, I call all members of my company by name.

Intern Who?

How would you feel if you were a nameless intern? Nurturing relationships with customers and vendors isn't everything—getting to know your peers (even interns), employees, and boss is just as important. Reaching out to other employees, regardless of what they do, creates trust and respect, and acknowledges that they are valued. Workers are real people with feelings, personalities, and problems. People need to know that what they do is integral to, and appreciated by, the company. From top to bottom, everyone likes to be acknowledged for a job well done. Every day, get to know the most valuable part of your business: the people.

If you want to win friends, make it a point to remember them. If you remember my name, you pay me a subtle compliment; you indicate that I have made an impression on you. Remember my name and you add to my feeling of importance.
—Dale Carnegie

Personal Space Wars: Office Edition

Personal space is a touchy subject, or not touchy, depending on if you're comfortable with a friendly pat on the back from your boss. The word says it best—personal space is personal. Whether you work in a cubicle, on a construction site, or in your own private office, you probably won't appreciate a co-worker sitting on your papers, ruffling your hair, or reaching over you to borrow your tape, saying, "Can I borrow this? Thanks."

Most of my advice to maintain feel-good relations between co-workers falls under general manners.

- Ask before taking, and say "please" and "thank you." You won't sound outdated, I promise. At least in the business world, manners are here to stay.
- Respect a person's cubicle, desk, or office.
- Don't judge other's decorations. Yes, I know you might think a Hello Kitty obsession is funny, but you wouldn't like someone else judging your personal style choices either.
- Remember that physical contact should be kept to a minimum.
- Using threatening or bullying language is a fast track to getting fired.

Think of your co-workers like a big family. You are STUCK with them, whether you like it or not. You don't have to like your co-workers, but please treat them with respect. Some co-workers will drive you up a wall, and you might never be "buddy-buddy," but being civil will make your work life tolerable.

Fun Fact: Presidential Space Invasion

On July 13th, 2006, President Bush invaded the personal space of Germany's first female Chancellor, Angela Merkel. During a G-8 meeting of world leaders, the President of the United States approached Merkel from behind and attempted a friendly shoulder massage. That's a nice gesture, right? Of course, but it's the highest order of UN-professional. Merkel tensed her shoulders and threw her arms up in surprise and professional discomfort! *Awkward...*

The Handshake

A handshake is universally accepted in most business practice as a sign of agreement, gratitude, politeness, respect, and mutual confidence (all really positive things, you see?). In fact, many consider it the ONLY acceptable physical contact between men and women in the professional world.

As an employer, my experience with handshakes ranges from the sublime to the utterly disgusting—yes, I've refused to shake a hand after its owner dug for lunch in her own nose!

A simple handshake goes a long way. Have you ever received an "iron death-grip" or a "dead fish" handshake? Remember this: A good handshake should be invisible. When thinking about you, a potential employer, new business partner, or prospective client shouldn't remember your handshake. A smooth, confident, "I know what I'm doing," handshake will be as natural and unnoticed as breathing. You want to be remembered for your confidence and potential, not for crushing someone's hand, or for seeming insecure and scared.

Five helpful tips for becoming a master hand-shaker:

1. Be natural—don't force it. If the time seems right, give it a go!

   A winning handshake:
   - is usually given standing, not sitting.
   - keeps the fingers close together with the thumb up.
   - lasts about 3 seconds maximum. Any longer becomes awkward.
   - is firm, but not overpowering or bone-breaking.
   - is clean—make sure your hands aren't wet, sticky, smelly, electrified, or worse!
   - ends after one or two "shakes," even if the introduction continues.
   - is given with good eye contact and active listening.

2. A handshake is acceptable in four main circumstances: on a first introduction, *"Hi, I'm Janice* (handshake). *Nice to meet you!";* at the time of leaving, *"It's been a pleasure!"* (handshake); when greeting guests; and whenever someone else extends a hand—don't leave a guy hanging!

3. Say something with your handshake. See what I did in #2? Verbal communication grabs attention, indicates *why* you are shaking hands, and is a sure way to avoid awkwardness.

4. To avoid a "wet" handshake, hold any drink you might have in the left hand, or simply dry your hand before proceeding. People will appreciate your consideration.

Note: There's nothing wrong with being left-handed, but since the majority of people shake hands with their right, left-handed people are at a slight disadvantage. If you primarily use your left hand, I suggest you practice shaking hands with your right—go through the motions until it feels natural.

Telephone Etiquette: Romancing the Phone

I don't mean this literally—no sexy-talk on the phone. Politeness and professionalism is the winning combination when dealing with caller clients. Often a phone call is a customer's first impression of your business. Believe it or not, email hasn't made phones go the way of the dinosaurs. In fact, a good old-fashioned phone call is what many businesses and customers prefer—it can put you worlds ahead of the competition. The reality is that phones are still a primary make-it-or break-it component of many business interactions, and proper etiquette is important whether you're a babysitter, a top executive, or an IRS call center associate.

Technically Speaking...

Remember that you're not paid to have an hour-long heart-to-heart with the client or customer. You provide a service. If making a tasteful joke or sharing a personal story is welcome, be my guest. In fact, personal connection can really enhance business communication, but you must start with a level of professional standard. A customer's time is valuable, and your time is valuable to your employer—make your phone call pleasant, helpful, and try not to waste anybody's time by staying focused with these general rules:

- **Use a professional voice**—customer casualness gets casual customers only. I've called businesses where the receptionist said, "Hey, what's up?" I'm not a casual customer—I hung up. Remember to give your customers a great first impression by using a professional voice and formal manner of speaking.
- **Be helpful and informative.** When answering calls, introduce yourself and your organization. For example, "Hello, Example Corporation, John speaking."
- **Respond to voice messages in a timely fashion.** An essential part of business is getting back to people who need your advice, service, or commitment.
- **Speaking slowly and clearly wins the race and the customer.** Mumbling, speaking too fast, or slurring your words will weaken your business relations. Also, no one likes to be yelled at, so keep from breaking eardrums with a moderate speaking voice.
- **Don't smack-chew-smack gum.** It's disrupting and obnoxious.
- **Don't use the speakerphone to answer an incoming call.**
- **When putting someone on hold, ask if it's all right first.** A few minutes on hold can seem like an eternity for any caller, so check in every 30 to 45 seconds to ask if he or she would like to continue holding or simply leave a message.

Boss/Employee Relationships

Keep your boss well informed of your activities. It's the best way to keep him or her in the loop, get timely feedback on your labor—perhaps the quickest way to a promotion?!

Communication is the simplest solution and most constructive way to handle this relationship. Some bosses can be hard to reach, hard of hearing, or even hard-headed, but a strong line of communication is the first step to understanding your boss and to doing the job he or she expects you to do. Try to discover if your boss is a "visual" or an "auditory" person. Does your boss prefer to read a report and flip through the charts, or perhaps it's best to give your boss a conversational summary of your projects? Is he or she more likely to answer an email or a phone call?

Always bear in mind where you stand on the totem pole. Never threaten your boss, attempt intimidation, or assert yourself as superior. Your boss has the power of "hiring and firing," which he or she will NOT soon let you forget.

When your boss errs, take a deep breath and tell yourself that everyone is human. We all make mistakes and have the occasional personal or financial disaster. Never talk to or email your boss when angry (a very bad idea). Remember that a supervisor or executive is responsible for a lot of people and fairness can't always be given to everyone.

Technological Blunders

New technology has created more office etiquette problems in the past decade than I can count. We'll make one really simple etiquette rule to live by.

TURN IT OFF.

I see a young professional I hired enter our company meeting with one earphone dangling from his head. The professional then proceeds to text throughout the meeting while I and other colleagues are presenting data. After returning to work, I find him perusing Facebook and uploading photos from his phone to Instagram.

What do you think happens to this young professional? Correct—Fired! No questions asked. Truth be told, that's a true story. I've also fired a person because her texting habit was destroying her productivity.

Here's the bottom line: technology such as mobile phones, tablets, and social media sites are distractions from work. My personal dislike of technology addiction is an etiquette issue—playing on your phone or listening to music during a meeting is just plain rude! You wouldn't pull out a John Grisham novel and start reading during a board meeting, would you? So why do some people think it's OK to break the common law of courtesy by reading and sending text messages? It's *not.*

Social Media: Getting a Bad Rap

Calling all users of Facebook, Myspace, Twitter, Youtube, and any other social media-sharing site! I want to tell you this now, so it doesn't give you a rude awakening when your boss calls you in to discuss the pictures you posted from that rave at Jimmy's house last weekend—EMPLOYERS WILL LOOK AT YOUR ONLINE PROFILES.

Your online social profiles, even if set to "private," are accessible by employers. Facebook, for one, sells the rights to your profile, making it legal and possible for employers to see what kind of image you're putting out into the cyber-social atmosphere.

What's Their Problem?

The image that you put out onto the internet is public information. An employer's main concern is that the things you do and say in cyberspace, especially if representative of the company, can hurt the business. Also, snooping on your profile gives employers an inside look at your personality and whether or not your "lifestyle" is one that fits the company's ethics—there's that big E word again.

Freshman Mistakes

As you know, college students love to have a good time, and even more, they like to show it off to their friends, especially on Facebook. Posting pictures from bars, house parties, or general pictures with alcohol present is a rookie mistake made by many college students. Fresh out of college with a crisply pressed degree, looking for that first job, many young professionals find that their college "lifestyles" don't suit the professional world. Many have been rejected, or fired, from jobs for inappropriate content placed on social media sites.

That's your fair warning.

Now, can we be Facebook friends? Add me…

International Etiquette

Aye, there's the rub. Etiquette, while based on ethics, is different in every country and culture. For example, Europeans shake hands MUCH more than Americans—surprised? In France, it is polite to greet a friend with kisses on both cheeks. Believe it or not, many countries don't follow the "time is money" mentality of North Americans—being hasty and disrespecting a social hour might lose you valuable business. As you travel the globe, etiquette for eating changes—chopsticks, or fork and spoon? Should I eat everything on my plate or leave a little untouched? Why did the Chinese businessman tell me to slurp my soup?

The idea is this: Business is GLOBAL. Somewhere along your business escapades, you'll make a deal with someone internationally. How will you greet them? How should you look, act, and stand? Should you bow? What can you expect from an international business partner? International etiquette is important to show that you are serious about an international business relationship.

The Truth

Business is about making friends, and when far from home, the proper etiquette can help. Etiquette *rules* might change depending on the country and the culture, but most people respond to the basics of *courtesy, consideration*, and *politeness.* Your responsibility is to understand the cultural and etiquette differences between yourself and your business partner. There is no Big Book of Etiquette for every international situation, but I suggest you brush up before contacting a Chinese manufacturer or traveling to Spain to meet your most valuable supplier.

Think about the following international etiquette practices from around the globe. Compare them to our own. Why do you use etiquette anyway, and what difference does it make that some countries do it differently?

In many Asian countries, a contract isn't binding law, but more like a legal formality that is heartily ignored if necessary. Asian businessmen often prefer business "relationships" and values such as trust, respect, and loyalty. For a long time, U.S. computer manufacturers couldn't make deals with the Japanese government because top executives pushed deals and contracts instead of first building solid international business relationships.

In Thailand, don't use a fork to put food in your mouth. Thais use a fork to push food onto the spoon, which is then used to eat. Chopsticks are only used for noodle dishes.

In the Middle East and parts of Africa, never eat with your left hand. The left hand is associated with "unsanitary fluids," therefore, it is disgusting to even touch your plate with your left hand.

When doing business in Europe, excluding England, you'll only deal with one currency, the Euro—no converting money in each new country. Simple, isn't it? The value of one Euro changes with the market, but *usually* stays at about $1.50 USD.

In Russia, never reject an offer of Vodka, especially in a business situation. The offering is a social act of goodwill, a sign of friendship, if you will. To say no, even if you don't usually drink, is considered bad manners. The only acceptable form of mixing (no ice!) is vodka with beer, which produces a kicker called "yorsh," an *interesting* substitute for your morning coffee.

In Japan, the placement of your chopsticks could really upset your host. The only proper place to set them is right in front of you, parallel with the edge of the table. Leaving your chopsticks straight up in your rice bowl is similar to a Japanese funeral custom—don't remind your host of a dead ancestor!

Latin American countries each have their own etiquette and cultural differences, but some business habits are shared:

- In all Latin American countries, except Brazil, you'll hear Spanish as the national language. Many businessmen speak English, but honoring the local language opens business doors.
- Latin American culture is often less strict about time, people often asking, "the English hour, or the Latin hour?" meaning "Should I be promptly on time, or does 6 p.m. mean I can mosey in at 6:30?"
- In most South American countries, business is often warm and social, just like Latin customs of hospitality, meaning that a healthy conversation and joking around is required before proper business can be discussed.
- Also, personal space is often smaller and conversations can be in quite close contact. Don't be surprised if a client or business associate stands uncomfortably close.
- In Mexico, one cannot do proper business without knowing the person. In Mexican business circles, knowing a person includes knowing his or her family. Especially for high circles of business, having a "family contact" introduce you can really speed things up.

Imagine you are an international businessman meeting an American for the first time. What customs might you find strange? What are some etiquette issues that you might not know?

Consideration

"Why," you might ask, "is etiquette so darn important?" Consideration for one's fellow man (be it customer, employee, boss, client, friend, whomever) makes business life a lot easier. When things go smoothly, a company is said to be "well oiled," with all parts in full swing. Etiquette ensures that people are civil, polite, and responsible to each other—you know, the big things in life. BUT if you learn the big things first, the nitty-gritty rules will be second nature—etiquette becomes easy.

A–Z Etiquette for Work

Annoyances (Co-workers)

Co-workers can either make your life pleasant or make you want to scream. Some people you just *can't* live with—remind yourself that you don't have to. Rise above an office conflict or an annoying co-worker, and express your dissatisfaction. Most small annoying habits are unintentional. That knuckle-cracker probably doesn't realize he is causing you mental anguish. The gum-chewer who's smacking away like there's no tomorrow will continue smacking unless you ask her to please stop.

Take a look at the following examples, and decide which is the most etiquette-proper way to say, "Stop," about whatever is bothering you.

"I brought that stapler from home. I don't mind you using it, but I would appreciate it if you ask my permission before taking it."

"If you don't stop cracking your knuckles, I'll crack them for you, if know what I mean!"

"I don't mean any offense, but you're making me kind of uncomfortable. I'm just not interested."

"I'd appreciate it if you would shut your big mouth and stop spreading rumors about me around the factory."

"Stop asking me out. I don't like you. I don't like your jokes, and I don't ever want to date you."

"Hey, I bought you this pack of gum because I know you like smacking in our ears."

"I know that I'm being picky, but I'd really appreciate it if you could chew your gum a little more discretely. I'm having trouble focusing."

It's pretty easy to spot the polite way to say it, but when you're furious, it might not be so easy to say. Try your best to be civil.

Apologies

For most business blunders, "Oops, my bad!" doesn't cut it. For minor offenses, like mistakenly eating someone's lunch out of the office refrigerator, a spoken apology will be just fine, if you're sincere. For major offenses such as slander, offensive remarks, or a breech of ethics, a spoken as well as formal, written apology letter is necessary.

Why Apologize? You Had Good Reason!

If you're getting fired for some "situation," why not just cut losses and leave quietly? Or perhaps you feel you did the right thing—why should you apologize? If it was an honest mistake, or just unfair finger-pointing, an apology letter can do several things. First, an apology gives you the high ground. Get out of the scuffle and rise above pettiness. Second, it can clarify the situation from your perspective, an important thing in office politics. Third, if you so choose, you can truly claim responsibility for your actions, something any employer can respect. And finally, don't burn bridges. An apology can promote continued healthy professional connections with your boss or co-workers.

Appointments

Treat your appointments with courtesy (remember that word?). When scheduling an appointment, make sure you value another's time. Work to set a firm time and date that is efficient for both parties. Waffling on a time is the quickest way to disrespect any busy businessperson.

On the morning of the appointment day, most businesses will confirm the appointment time. If you've set up an appointment through a secretary, call the business to confirm. It is good etiquette to do so. Does your dentist's office call to confirm your appointments? Mine does, and I always appreciate the reminder; otherwise, my teeth would never get cleaned!

Honor your appointment, be on time (or early), and properly thank him for meeting. If you must cancel for any reason, inform the contact as soon as possible. In this case, a personal phone call with an explanation would be well appreciated.

Burping (Belching)

Occasionally, you just can't stand the pressure, and a burp pops up. I can't, with clear conscience, tell you to suppress a burp (that's uncomfortable and unhealthy), but there is a polite way to burp around your co-workers. Please, squelch your burp as much as humanly possible, and cover your mouth with your hand or napkin. Excuse yourself immediately after, and explain how bell peppers don't settle well.

Black Tie

Most of your casual business parties will not be "black tie," but if you rub elbows with elite business professionals, you could easily be invited to a "black tie" event. This simply means tuxedo attire, black tie included.

Boss/Employee Relationships

These are very likely the most important relationships you can form in a professional career. Bosses can take almost any form in the imagination. You might see your boss as a greedy dragon, a harmless teddy bear, or the Wizard of Oz working magic strings behind the scenes. For your sake, I sincerely hope the bosses you encounter will set a good example, become mentors as you grow professionally, and be people whose relationships you carry on through life.

Briefcase

A briefcase is a status symbol accessory, usually used by businesspeople. Whether or not you carry a briefcase depends on what business you are in. If other people on the same rung of the career ladder are carrying briefcases, you can assume it's safe to ditch the backpack and upgrade professionally. If you are a journalist, canvas bags are often a popular accessory; photographers have professional camera cases; lawyers often carry conservative leather cases. Regardless, you want to carry something that fits your professional life in style, status, and functionality.

Business Card

Is a business card an unnecessary formality? Most professionals will say NO! A business card can be used by almost anyone—it is a physical calling card to accompany your professional personality. Even if you make a stellar "can't be forgotten" first impression, handing over your business card conveniently locates your name, professional services, and your contact information for later use. Cards are a rather handy, old-fashioned business solution.

Style Tips

Most successful business cards are simple, straightforward, and sometimes elegant. Flashy logos and decorative designs seem eye-catching, but they are usually distracting and unnecessary, unless you are entering an artistic field where your card might be seen as a sample of your work.

Stephanie Skinner
Media Consultant
Edge Enterprises, Inc

1975 Loop Drive
Turin, Georgia 33840
Telephone: 784-293-0912

A Standard Format:

Name, profession, Company Name, and business contact information.

Note: Personal (home) phone numbers are not usually included on business cards.

Business Gift

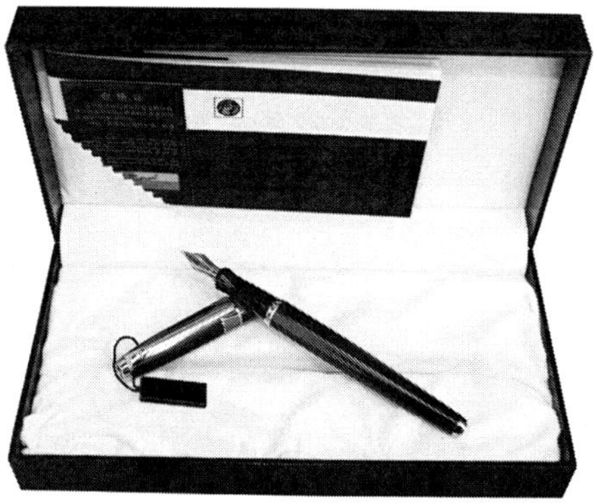

Nobody rejects a gift. Giving a small gift to your co-workers or your boss is not usually expected, but a nice thing to do. Company gift exchanges can a fun way to break the normal routine.

If you give your boss a gift, don't give anything lavish or personal that could be considered bribery or general "teacher's pet" behavior. It's best to wait for an occasion where your boss has already given you a gift, so you can better judge what is appropriate.

Business Writing Style

No interpreters or translation should be required for business writing. Plain English is best. Good business writing is direct, straightforward, yet polite. It should be well organized with main ideas and subtopics. Avoid rambling or getting sidetracked. Be direct—"I enclose" and "Thank you for…". The same clear writing that you use in reports and business correspondence should also be used in memos and presentations.

Condolence Note

Remember, it's the thought that counts. In the case of a death of a business associate, employee, or even if one of their family members passes, it is good etiquette to send a condolence note to the survivors expressing your regret.

Coughing and Sneezing

Coughing and sneezing are similar to belching. Did you know a sneeze has a blast radius of fifteen feet? It might sound strange, but it's best to sneeze into your elbow—turn away from people nearby, and then apologize. If you have an uncontrollable fit of coughing, leave the room until the fit subsides. If you are legitimately sick, consider taking a sick day! Your co-workers will appreciate you keeping your germs to yourself.

Eating at Work

I don't know about you, but I work better with food for thought. Check with your management about the policies of eating while working. Usually, small snacks are acceptable (don't be a "crumby" worker), while full meals at your desk get messy. Most of workplaces have a break room where you can take lunch or get refreshments. You might even make friends around the office if you share your snack-time delights.

Email Etiquette

I live by email—what was business like without it? It was certainly a lot SLOWER! Beware slopping some words together and hitting "send" without giving it a second thought. Email experts agree, your email identity can make or break your professional connections.

Take a look at these quick tips for being professional with proper email etiquette:

- Briefly introduce yourself if not already clear. Don't assume the recipient knows who you are or what you want.
- Keep a grammar reference book nearby, and use it to keep track of confusing usage like "than" and "then," or "alright" and "all right."
- Save the "smileys" for your special someone. Emoticons, slang, jargon, and abbreviated words like "probs" for "probably" and "k" for "okay," should probs be omitted.
- Always include a subject line that best describes the purpose of your email. Obviously, you wouldn't write "Bananas, Bananas, Bananas" if your email were about corporate finances.
- Only discuss public matters. Email, however hidden or protected, can get "leaked" one way or another. Private material can become public humor in a single click.
- Confidential information should not be sent via email. It can easily fall into the wrong hands.
- Respond in a timely fashion. I know it's easy to read an email and forget about it. Instead, read it, reply thoroughly, and be done with it.

Gossip Through the Grapevine

Co-workers are like close-knit families—everyone knows everyone else's business. Word spreads quickly about business politics like firings or someone getting passed over for a promotion. Likewise, grapevine gossip is unavoidable, and rumors spread like wildfire through the cubicles. My general suggestion is to rise above it. Listen to gossip if you have to, but don't bet your house on anything you hear. Certainly, don't pass gossip on—be the end of the line.

Hiring and Firing

Accepting a job offer requires a formal acceptance letter, proof that you accepted.

Firing comes with it's own etiquette. Large management corporations may be rather impersonal, issuing a simple notice of termination. Most firing scenarios will be done face-to-face with an explanation of "why" the company can no longer keep you as an employee. Some of the most common reasons are budget constraints, downsizing, personality conflict, or a position becoming unnecessary. Firing is such a sensitive subject, we've come up with easier ways to say it, such as, "you're getting terminated, canned, axed, laid off, discharged, dismissed," or simply, "we're letting you go."

Introductions

Yourself: Introduce yourself briefly with just your name, "Hello, I'm Dave Cranford..." and if appropriate to the situation, include your profession, "...the coroner for Washington County. Nice to meet you." If you immediately forget a person's name, ask again, before too long, with an apology. "I'm sorry, I missed your name the first time. What was it again?" Introducing yourself to co-workers, business associates, and anybody else quickly breaks the ice and integrates everybody into a better team and work environment.

Others: Imagine you meet with several different potential clients to discuss a project. You already know everyone attending, but the others have never met. You should first introduce everyone with a quick synopsis of who they are and what their role in your project will be. Be brief, courteous, and ask if each person would like to say something about themselves and what they are contributing.

Don't forget to relax, smile, and let your funny bone show. Business is a human interaction; otherwise, we'd program robots to conduct our boring business meetings while we kicked back in an easy chair!

Lunch Etiquette

Lunch is a social time to talk, enjoy a meal, and, of course, do business! Lunch Etiquette depends on who you are: the host or the guest. The host is responsible for choosing the restaurant and providing a comfortable atmosphere in which to talk (one that matches your client's taste), managing the meeting and deciding when to talk business (usually before eating and never during), and paying for the meal, usually with a credit card to avoid fumbling with cash. As the host, you want to handle the lunch as unobtrusively as possible. As the guest, sit back and enjoy yourself. Make sure to be courteous, and represent yourself and your business with refined manners and good taste. Talk business when it's time to talk business, and relax during the small talk.

Lying, Cheating, Stealing
Etiquette takes all of its tips from Ethics, and these three aren't ethical at all. Lying, cheating, and stealing are discourteous and inconsiderate, if not always illegal.

Meetings
If you looked into a professional meeting room in full swing, you'd just see a bunch of people listening to another person speak. But you'd miss all the details. A meeting room is often ordered by hierarchy—the highest-ranking official conducting the meeting sits at the head of the table with a personal assistant close by. A president or board member usually controls the meeting by giving information and allowing others the opportunity to present or share information with the other team members. One person is usually responsible for the "minutes" of the meeting (a written record of all conversation topics, decisions, and statements). As always, "politeness" is the key word. Respectfully give your attention to the speaker, as you would like them to do the same for you.

Resignation
Formal resignation is best done face-to-face with the person responsible for your work, in most cases, your immediate boss. Higher executives will make a public announcement. In addition to your oral resignation, a signed and sealed letter explaining and confirming your resignation is the correct course of action.

Sexual Harassment
Not only is sexual harassment crude, disgusting, and unethical, it's also illegal. You might be unaware of what constitutes sexual harassment, but the law doesn't tolerate ignorance. Lewd comments, jokes, or inappropriate touching all fall under sexual harassment territory. In short, it occurs when some sexualized action interferes with work performance or creates an intimidating, hostile, or offensive work environment.

All of the following examples are considered sexual harassment:

- Unwanted jokes, sexual references, or offensive words on clothing
- Touching (other than a handshake) or unwanted body contact such as grabbing of the waist, slapping on the bottom, or moving to block a person's path to escape
- Unrelenting requests for dates that are repeatedly rejected
- Making public any sexually suggestive pictures, objects, or graphics
- Sending or posting emails with sexually charged or offensive material or language

"The power play" is a common form of sexual coercion, which is also harassment. It's a sad world that someone in power considers a high position as permission to demand sexual favors or speak to his or her employees in a sexually demeaning manner. Many receptionists and secretaries may encounter this problem. If you feel that you could be a victim of sexual harassment, seek help, seek advice, and consult with your company's counselor.

Disclaimer: Most flirting is NOT sexual harassment. Before you go yelling "harassment" all the way to the Human Resource Department, make sure you feel uncomfortable enough to risk someone else his/her job.

Sharing

When does sharing become "taking?" Imagine you're one of two electricians working at a diaper factory. When you switch shifts, the other electrician uses your tools. You confront him about it, and he says, "Didn't you ever learn to share?" Who is right? In general, sharing is good, but remember to respect another person's property. Asking first is only right.

Small Talk

Making small talk can seem like a BIG challenge. The easiest way I've ever seen it described was in a book by Phyllis Davis entitled *E2: Using the Power of Ethics and Etiquette in American Business.* She suggests the 30-day rule: small talk should only cover things that have happened 30 days in the past or will happen 30 days in the future. Try to steer clear of discussions about office politics, irrelevant business talk, or company policy.

For example, your boss has asked you to meet with her for a business lunch. Use the 30 day rule to make small talk when awkward silence threatens. Talking points include:

- That yoga class you're signed up to start next week.
- The promotion your mom just received.
- The project your brother is completing to become an Eagle Scout.
- The company softball game you all won last week.
- Your recent move to a new neighborhood.

Small talk is important for most social interactions. Very rarely will you form the kind of relationship where "everything is shared," including your private life drama and personal aspirations. Most work-talkers are small-talkers and forming friendly relationships with your co-workers depends upon this crucial skill.

Stationery

Most businesses have stationery paper with the company "letterhead" at the top. This stationery is used for professional business contact outside of the company, including emails to important business associates. Rule to Remember: *Never do personal business on the company's letterhead.*

Thank You Notes

The best job seekers know a thing or two about "thank you" notes. These are important to send on several occasions, including following an interview or after receiving a business gift. Sending a thank you note to an interviewer is a wonderful way to remind him/her of your name, and it suggests that you consider the position an important prospect. Thank you notes also show your character, consideration, and the employee initiative. Many employers say that thank you notes are one of the most beneficial, but overlooked, traditions in the workplace.

XYZ *(eXamine Your Zipper...and Your Dress)*

Standing up for a presentation with an open fly can be rather embarrassing. Would you appreciate a co-worker pulling you aside and saying, "Hey, your fly is unzipped." The general rule is "Do unto others as you would have them do unto you," so help a co-worker out by quietly informing him that his attire needs etiquette attention.

The same goes for women. I think you know how embarrassing it is to go in public clueless that your dress is slightly see-through, or that you're showing too much thigh because your dress is caught in your underwear. Again, help a girl out. Ignorance is bliss until it becomes embarrassing.

Bibliography

All I Ever Need to Know I Learned in Kindergarten
By Robert Fulghum
Villard Books, New York, NY
©1988
A humorous and touching book about one man's realization about all the really *important* things in life!

E²--Using the Power of Ethics and Etiquette in American Business
By Phyllis Davis
Entrepreneur Media
©2003
This book has highly helpful tips on how to be ethical and etiquette conscious in the business world.

Ethics: Selections From Classical & Contemporary Writers
by Oliver A. Johnson
Holt, Rinehart & Winston, Inc.
©1989
This is a college-level textbook that takes a look at classical authors, such as Socrates, and investigates some of the arguments behind modern systems of ethics.

The New Etiquette: Real Manners for Real People in Real Situations—An A-To-Z Guide
By Marjabelle Young Stewart
St. Martin's Griffin, New York, NY
©1987
All you'll ever need to know about Etiquette is in this book. From business etiquette to planning a wedding.

Values in Action
by Carol Eliot, Elizabeth Orens and Penny Work
©1992
Council for Religion in Independent Schools, Washington, D.C.
Here's an in-depth guide to teaching middle-schoolers about ethics. Outlines an interactive program for flexing those value-specific mental muscles!

Carole Marsh's **CAREERS CURRICULUM**™

FOR MIDDLE SCHOOL, HIGH SCHOOL, COLLEGE AND **BEYOND!**

"If you are ready for 'readiness'...for choosing a career pathway... deciding what to do after high school...or for a first job, or raise and promotion - THIS SERIES IS FOR YOU!"

– James Barnard

Job Tracks: 60* Great Careers and How to Get from Where You Are... to Where You Want To Go!

This book is filled with unique and effective approaches for helping students find their career pathway! Featuring 60 careers from today's job market, this book allows young people to hear first-hand from a person with the job: how they got it, what they do, what education and skills were required, and "what I would have done differently!" Readers get the feel of what particular careers might actually be like—essential knowledge for that all-important decision!

"Entertaining and charming to read!"

Essential Skills for the Real World of Work: Things EVERY Student Must Know!

There's no other book that does a better job of sharing essential skills for the real business world and explaining why they are essential! This book dishes out the subtleties, nuances, and in-between-the-lines considerations of job interviewers who are not only interested in candidates with essential skills, but are actually desperate for them! It includes a fun and effective scoring system to encourage students to rack up job-readiness skills long before they are required.

"Highly encouraging and enlightening!"

Would You Hire This Person? A Look at Getting Hired (or Not!)...from the Point of View of Your (Possible!) Future Employer

Read verbatim interviews that are both entertaining and enlightening! In this book, students hear both sides of the interview, including the employer and job candidate's unspoken thoughts. The reader can decide for himself or herself if they would hire the job candidate before learning the actual outcome.

"Such realistic scenarios – I got nervous reading them! I wanted the person to get the job, but, gee...I can see why some would not!"

www.careerscurriculum.com

Work Words: Job/Business/Career Words & Terms You Need to Know!

Get ready for lots of insider information and a few inside jokes! Written by a real employer, this book defines essential job, business, and career words and terms with insight, humor, and pizzazz! The contents of the book are organized into entertaining and effective groupings.

"Why be embarrassed when you can be empowered by knowing 'job speak' BEFORE you even get the job?"

Business Ethics & Etiquette for Students: You MUST Know These!

This highly entertaining and immensely practical book is an eye-opening must-read for students and new hires! It provides them with the confidence to avoid embarrassment, misstep, lost opportunity, and more.

"Fascinating and quite a lot of material covered. Anyone can benefit from this double-whammy of info book!"

The Parent and Teacher's Guide: Helping Students Navigate the Bumpy Road from School to More School, First Job, and Career

Filled with candid help from someone who has traveled the bumpy road of "non-readiness" from school to job to career, this book boasts timely and honest information that will help kids get ready for the real world of work. The wealth of ideas available to parents and teachers in this book will help them to navigate their student's journey ahead!

"Marsh has a keen sense of devotion to every type of student truly seeking a path to success. This book is worth the price for the compassion and humor, explanation of 'Rigor vs. Rigor Mortis,' and 'Why Study These Subjects' section. She's clearly 'been there, done that,' and achieved great success despite many obstacles!"

Carole Marsh's CAREERS CURRICULUM™

PLEASE CONTINUE TO VISIT OUR WEBSITE FOR MORE K-12 PRODUCTS IN PRINT & ONLINE FORMATS, INCLUDING:

- INDIVIDUAL CAREER MANUAL
- SCHOOL INFORMATION SHEETS
- COMPANY PROFILE SHEETS
- MAP OF OPPORTUNITIES
- ESSENTIAL SKILLS PASSPORT BOOK

... AND MUCH MORE!!

FOR MIDDLE SCHOOL, HIGH SCHOOL, COLLEGE AND **BEYOND!**

www.careerscurriculum.com